Own Your Future

Overcoming Negative Emotional Tendencies
and Attaining Your Financial Goals

I0067379

Own Your Future

Overcoming Negative Emotional Tendencies
and Attaining Your Financial Goals

Dan Cairo

YouSpeakIt
PUBLISHING
*The Easy Way
to Get Your Book
Done Right*™

Copyright © 2019 Dan Cairo

All rights reserved. No part of this book may be reproduced or transmitted in any form or by any means without written permission of the publisher, except in the case of brief quotations embedded in critical articles and reviews.

This material has been written and published solely for educational purposes. The author and the publisher shall have neither liability nor responsibility to any person or entity with respect to any loss, damage, or injury caused or alleged to be caused directly or indirectly by the information contained in this book.

Statements made and opinions expressed in this publication are those of the author and do not necessarily reflect the views of the publisher or indicate an endorsement by the publisher.

ISBN: 978-1-945446-65-8

To my mother, Juliana, who is the greatest mother I ever could have been blessed to have. You turned this shy little boy into the man he is today and showed me what unconditional love truly is. To my father, Bill, who taught me the value of hard work and sacrifice. You both preached never to compromise my character and always put family first. You both will be forever in my mind, my heart, and my soul.

To my sister, Sandi, whom I kid way too much but love with all my heart. You are such a wonderful and caring person, and I am so lucky to have you in my life. To my nieces, Olivia and Claire, who are such wonderful and caring young ladies, I love you so much; and to Ray, who is all a brother-in-law I can ever hope to have and such an important person in our family.

To my children, Austin, Adam, and Karina, who have given me such a kaleidoscope of emotions. You all have such kind hearts; I want you to live in the moment and be gentle in your thoughts and fierce in your goals.

And, finally, to my beautiful wife, Cindy, who is my perfect soul mate, and who has always shown me what having a wonderful and giving heart truly is. I would not have arrived at this moment without your loyalty, faith, and love.

In Loving Memory of Juliana Cairo
December 26, 1932–November 22, 2018

The pain of your loss is immense, but I'd gladly have my heart in pain than never having you, Mama. I am what I am because of you. I love how I love because you showed me how.

Forever in my soul and always in my thoughts,

I will smile when I see a butterfly floating in the breeze.

Forever my #1 girl.

Contents

CHAPTER FIVE

Acknowledgments

I would like to acknowledge Donny, Prab, Craig, Heidi, and AnneMarie, who, in spite of working with me day after day, are truly family; and all the incredible industry advisors that I have had the privilege to work beside who have helped mold me into the professional that I try to be every day.

To all my friends: We have created a village to raise our children, travel, and have amazing times together. We continue to write new chapters, and we are all so blessed to be in each other's lives.

And, finally, to my clients, who have no idea what their fellowship means to me: For many, your lives have been an open book of which I am blessed to be a small part. I have learned as much from you as hopefully you have from me, and I thank you for your trust and loyalty in what I do.

Introduction

*You can attain your financial goals in spite of yourself
if you embrace behavioral change.*

Dear Reader,

I have written this book from a financial advisor's outlook on behavioral finance. I have more than thirty years' experience as a financial consultant, supervisor, and trainer of financial representatives, with a BFA designation (Behavioral Financial Advisor). I study people's behavior pertaining to how they make financial decisions. This book is an examination of people's behavioral paths, their current tendencies, and how they overcome negative tendencies to create a successful financial future.

People don't make bad decisions mathematically; they make bad decisions emotionally. When you ask somebody finance questions, you can see their physiology change as they become uncomfortable talking about it. At times, you may get a short dismissive response, and other times they will joke about their finances because they are uncomfortable. To be successful in finance, you need to strip away the uncomfortable emotions that go with it so you can help your clients make sound financial decisions for their future. But, they must first understand themselves.

Going to a financial advisor should not be like going to a proctologist. It should not be that uncomfortable. Talking to a financial advisor should be like talking to a confidant, a mentor, or a friend. That is what a financial advisor should be, and that's what I try to be to my clients.

Being *real* to my clients means we can have open conversations; they know that I'm an open book when they are talking to me. They can ask me anything, and I will give them an honest answer. They may not like the answer, but they are going to get an honest one.

I expect honesty in return. That's the only way we can partner together to create a successful journey toward financial independence and their individual financial goals.

Investors may not realize when we first meet that I'm just an average guy with the same fears and insecurities as any other person. Personally, I feel that one skill I've had since childhood is owning my weaknesses. I didn't get upset with others; I accepted the fears, anxieties, and lack of confidence that were within me.

That meant I had to change my path and not rely on others to guide me. As a child, I was horribly shy and lacked confidence, to a point that was debilitating. To this day, I continue to fight the person I was in order to become the vision of my authentic self in the future.

As is true for any a good trainer, mentor, or advisor, my job is not to make a client dependent on me, but to be independent of me. If people become dependent on helpers, they never change. You must become independent. That is the first step in changing. In other words: don't look to your past as a crutch.

Read this message with an open mind and an open heart. If need be, fight against the tendency to dismiss it.

You are deserving of happiness and success.

If you find yourself feeling not worthy, stop and ask yourself why or, should I say, why not?

Very few people talk about why they are falling short and why they are making the same kind of mistakes. In this book, I help you learn to tap into these emotions of planning, reflect on where you can improve, and see the benefit that can come from changing them.

Embrace change and be enthusiastic in life. If you're enthusiastic with the people that you know and, more importantly, those that you don't, and if you foster relationships and treat people well, you start creating positive energy that can propel you to wonderful experiences.

If, on the other hand, you stay at home all day because you have no money or you don't feel worthy, you're selling yourself short, and you're missing out on wonderful experiences.

CHAPTER ONE

Emotional Beginnings for Decision Making

OUR PREDISPOSITION

In my years of being a financial advisor, I have worked with many families. Parents tell me how vastly different their children are from one another in personality and in their belief systems, even though they were brought up in the same household. Within the same family, one child may grow up to be successful but another may not. Some kids are motivated; others are not. Some are outgoing; others are introverted and shy.

This situation played out in my own family growing up. I was an introvert, shy, almost timid. My sister came out from the womb swinging; it's ironic that she doesn't talk to people for a living as much as I do. Now, I'm the one who is hosting seminars, speaking in public, and talking to people, yet I was the one who was always fearful and tongue-tied.

I think people have a predisposition to who they are, but they also have the ability to change if they want to. A lot depends on upbringing and their willingness to challenge themselves.

Introvert or Extrovert

In many pre-K and kindergarten groups, there's at least one popular child holding court who draws attention from the other children. Then, there are one or more children who are content to play alone and follow the crowd. These children are not likely central members of the group but part of it.

Many extroverts have no issues with speaking — maybe even speaking their mind, whether or not they are correct. You hear them. Introverts, on the other hand, may keep their feelings, their thoughts, and desires to themselves, hoping that somebody asks them.

If a financial advisor doesn't ask the right questions — such as what are goals, objectives, and what's truly important — they are not going to get the right answers. If a person can't tell you honestly what their true definition of financial success is, as an advisor, you run the risk of placing that person in the same box that they have placed themselves for their whole life. Even worse, an advisor runs the risk of creating a cookie-cutter investment plan that is not unique to that particular client's goals and objectives.

A person must feel free to relate what they want and feel confident in asking questions. Everybody is entitled to go after their goals, objectives, and desires. Introverts may have to come out of their comfort zones, but that's not necessarily a bad thing. They simply need to acknowledge the discomfort. Over time, the discomfort may lessen.

For those who are more extroverted, they may need to spend more time listening and try to spend less time talking to reach success. Being opinionated can be a detriment in some cases, if unlike a financial advisor, they don't have the knowledge or access to up-to-date information.

While introverts may have to make a concerted effort to be heard, they need to strive to trust their opinions and take the chance to voice them in order to reach their desired level of success.

Happy or Angry

Since we have already talked about predisposition, I think that in early life, your environment has a lot to do with how you develop from your DNA. What I mean by this is that depending on their environment, an extrovert has the potential to become an angry person. For example, parents might curtail that person from speaking. When a child hears *be quiet* too often, it becomes a basis of frustration and, in some cases, aggression.

In my experience, the worst thing an advisor can do when a person is talking is to cut them off. They will become angry; you must give them an opportunity to express themselves.

Conversely, what is going to make an introvert happy?

Make them feel safe and supported. Ask the right probing questions so they feel it's okay to express themselves.

Most parents parent by accident. The biggest mistake I've seen is that they try to raise their child as they wish they had been raised, instead of trying to understand the child and provide an environment where children feel safe to communicate. That doesn't mean having no boundaries; it simply means to try to understand the little person in front of you and tailor your conversation to their personality type.

Fearful or Daring

As I mentioned in the introduction, I grew up timid and shy. People who met me would say: *Oh yeah, I don't think so.* Everybody goes through life in monumental moments; as a child, if you choose to embrace what is thrown at you, overcoming obstacles becomes easier.

I'll never forget my fourth-grade teacher, Mrs. Rivera. I found out later that she talked to my mom about how to bring me out of my shell. She made me do a recital of an Edgar Allen Poe play that I had to try out for with another young boy. The other young boy was a natural. First of all, he looked like he came out of an Edgar Allen Poe play.

I went home and cried, and I told my mom that I couldn't do it, that I didn't want to do it.

My mom said, "Listen to Mrs. Rivera. She believes in you. Be prepared. Study. Know your lines."

I did the recital and tried out for the part; I didn't get it, but I survived it.

That experience taught me that it was okay to fail, but you must try. You will always fail if you fail to try. That was monumental in my existence to realize that most obstacles that people put in front of themselves are self-induced. They're not real. It's all in their heads.

You need to acknowledge the discomfort, but don't let it beat you in your future walks of life and in your beliefs. You can change your belief system. You just need to take a chance on yourself to do so.

As a young kid, I was such a scaredy-cat. I haven't forgotten to this day the bully across the street; we'll call him Johnny. He was about four years older than I was, and he would pick on me all the time. Once, he picked me up, threw me in a trashcan, and smacked me around. It was humiliating. When I was outside playing, I would run inside the moment he came out.

My dad finally told me, "You know what, son? You need to stand up for yourself. If you're going to take a beating, take a beating, but it's going to prove to him that you're just not going to sit there and be pushed around. If you don't do that, there are going to be other Johnnys as you grow older. It might be in your school or when you get older in your workplace. A bully at whatever age may take your happiness or even your career. But you have to stand up for yourself."

I'll never forget that conversation or those words. So, one day as I was playing outside, I saw Johnny running down the street at me.

As he approached, I told myself: *Not this time,* and I just stood there.

He said, "Oh, so you're not running this time."

I said, "Not this time."

Let's put it this way—we had it out. After I beat the heck out of him, I ran home—a little excited, I told my dad, "I beat up Johnny."

My dad smiled and said, "I'm not proud of you for beating up Johnny. I'm proud of you for standing up for yourself."

That told me that my dad believed in me as my mom and Mrs. Rivera did. It comes down to having the ability to look in the mirror and seeing in yourself what other people see in you. That makes all the difference.

HOW WE ARE RAISED

It's important to understand that as children grow up, they are moldable. I have seen people I have known from childhood grow into adults who haven't changed at all. I have seen others who have made a wonderful transformation. Others figure out who they are later in life.

I think that as part of the evolution of a person, environment is fairly critical.

Are people being recognized for the value they have in various scenarios, whether it's a group setting, a work environment, or during childhood?

Too many times, people place value on what others can do for them, but the way to express value to others is recognizing who they are, their strengths, and their weaknesses. We are all individuals deserving respect.

For example, many wonderful clients are gay, but they grew up in restrictive environments. For many, the pressure from parents, relatives, and friends was so stifling that they tried to live a straight lifestyle, got married, and in many cases had children. As the years went on, they ended up divorced and settled into the lifestyle they were meant to have from the beginning.

Often, the pressure from parents is due to a lack of understanding or worrying more about what others may say instead of simply loving their child for who they are. Also, I feel there is a lack of flexibility in truly seeing the person in front of you.

Are you guilty of putting everyone in a box based on the box you feel comfortable in?

Are you willing to step outside your box and allow others to express themselves?

When it comes to finance, people make the same mistake over and over because they place themselves in a box. They don't look outside the box, which leads to repeating the same mistakes, but they can't understand why they are always in the same position.

Failure to see further than the tip of one's nose can be referred to as *eyes wide shut*. People may think they are in tune with their surroundings, the people around them, and the decisions they make. However, typically they make decisions based on the box they have placed themselves in.

That's how they'll flourish because they are creating their own momentum. Likewise, you create an environment where it's okay for you to step outside your box to succeed. You create your own momentum. If you continue to place yourself in a box of limitations, you will have limited growth. If you break out of your box, you flourish because you create your own momentum. Strive to create an environment where it's okay for you to step outside your box to succeed.

My job, the job of any good financial advisor, is to be supportive of the decisions that are being made. Nobody wants to fail. You could have a disagreement, but typically a disagreement with respect to goals and objectives is based on wanting the same things despite having different ways of communicating.

For example, after establishing goals and objectives and looking at a client's current financial situation, I may see that their current portfolios may be too conservative, thus preventing them from achieving their financial goals. Or, it may be too aggressive, which in a large market downturn, can create a setback as well. If I make a recommendation to be more conservative or a tad more aggressive, a person's personality may get in the way of success.

Were You Recognized for Who You Are?

Children often misunderstand who their parents are or what they are trying to accomplish. As a kid growing up, I played a lot of sports, but that was because my mom threw me into sports, not because my dad threw the ball with me.

My dad was a laborer. He didn't graduate from high school, and he never made more than $30,000 a year. He worked in factories, loading trucks. He was a rough guy who grew up in Kenosha, Wisconsin, and being unlearned, everything was black and white to him. He worked, and his wife raised the family — a traditional Italian household. He would come home, give my mom the paycheck, and didn't want the kids to bother him.

As I was growing up, I was envious of my friends' dads. I vowed to be active with my kids when the time came.

It wasn't until my dad passed that I saw him for who he was in the later stages of his life. While he wasn't the father who threw the ball, he was the family's protector.

There was always food on the table. There were always gifts under the Christmas tree.

He would have done anything for his family. He was faithful to his wife, and he was a pretty awesome guy and great role model. I didn't recognize the person he was because, like most children, I wanted more. He wasn't able to verbalize his love, but what I didn't recognize was that his actions showed his love for his family. The verbal love I received was from my mom.

My mom recognized who I was and gave me the ability to evolve into the person I am today. In any household, I think it's important for children to be recognized for who they are as individuals.

In other words, how beautiful is a diamond that is not yet harvested, cut perfectly, and polished?

Not very — and the same holds true for our children.

Flexible Upbringing

As far as being flexible with upbringing, every child should have the opportunity to grow up to be the person that they are intended to be. A parent's job is to provide guidelines along the path, not choose the path for their children to follow. You can't make somebody be who they're not.

When I tried sports back in the third grade, I was so shy I didn't even want to change for gym class. My sister and I went to a parochial school, and Mom worked in the school's cafeteria. Because I was so shy and wouldn't change at school for gym class, my mom would pick me up, take me home to change, and take me back to play sports.

Now, maybe that's taking flexibility to a whole different level, but that's what she was willing to do. If she hadn't done that, I likely wouldn't have played sports. But, because she did, I found my aggressive self excelled in sports. That's something I may not have discovered about myself had my mother not been as flexible as she was.

How Were You Managed?

Trying and excelling in sports in elementary and junior high school allowed me to continue with sports through high school, where I also excelled. But more than that, being active in sports showed me the value of being a leader. I had responsibilities in sports, and I learned to be a good teammate, get along with others, and support others.

Sports also taught me how to overcome obstacles — losing, missing a shot, or any number of other mishaps that can take place during a game. Everything that I learned through my athletics I might not have learned if my mom hadn't been flexible with me when I was in elementary school.

I now use all these values when running my own company — teamwork and working with my clients, to name a couple. I assure clients that even if they failed in the past, it's okay; we just need to move forward and make intelligent decisions. I tell them to not dwell on past poor decisions because that's in the past.

I say: *Let's make better choices today and in the future.*

It's unlikely I would have been successful as an advisor if I didn't have parents who recognized my insecurities as a child and helped me overcome them.

By being flexible with your children, you allow them to flourish. You allow them to have a safe place to make decisions, good or bad, because as a parent you're there to help pick up the pieces and provide encouragement should they fall. They will be encouraged to get back up, dust off their knees, and continue to learn how to make better decisions going forward.

To move forward in life, to become the best version of you, look in the mirror and know that you have worth, regardless of your insecurities, and that you have the ability to change if you want to. You deserve success.

Many don't realize that as you bridge that gap from childhood to adolescence, you decide whether you stay in the same box that you were born into or become a better person tomorrow than you are today. If you're uneasy or unhappy, please keep in mind that everybody has the ability to change if they want to.

FIGHT OR FLIGHT

Life is about overcoming challenges and obstacles. As I've told my children, sometimes bad things happen to good people. That's a given. It's how you react that will demonstrate the character that you have.

I think every person on God's planet could point to a frightening event or incident as a child that they never want to go through again. The fear could be a bully. It could be death. It could be speaking on a stage. You need to learn to recognize that fear for what it is and know that, nine times out of ten, the fearful result is manufactured in your mind.

Early Recollections

Children may be fearful of going into the water — whether in a swimming pool or at the lake. Or perhaps they're fearful of the needles at the doctor's office. Many times, the fear is unfounded and created in our mind.

It's no different than when a child has a bad experience with another child.

At the youngest of ages, what can another child do besides bully?

This is a real concern. But we must find the ability to recognize fear and pain and still move forward. We need to learn not to let fear prevent us from moving forward, and instead use it to motivate us.

I think the biggest problem with our youth is they would rather run away from something that makes them feel uncomfortable than meet it head-on. It's only by meeting an obstacle head-on that you can truly overcome it, regardless of what it is.

Relive the Feeling

When people have bad experiences, whether it's fear or humiliation, they bury them. *I never want to think about it again* is a common quote. I disagree.

I think the only way that you can improve yourself is to relive that fear. You want to relive that humiliation because you want to have it so embedded in your mind that you never go through it again in reality. That's the only way you can learn.

If we don't remember history, we are doomed to repeat it. It's the same thing in your mind emotionally.

If another person humiliates you, and you just forget about it because it's too painful to accept, who's to say it won't happen again?

You start creating a pattern of failure and of disrespecting yourself.

Here's a perfect example that I remember like it was yesterday: second-grade PE class. I was tall for my age. There was this little guy — about half my size, a total bully who walked around the school as if he owned it. We were out in the yard about to play basketball.

To my recollection, when the teams were being picked, he said, "Cairo, go sit down, we don't want you to play."

Like a little baby, I went and sat down and watched everybody else play basketball. I was not mad at him, but maybe I'm just programmed a little differently. I was upset at myself for not playing because another person had told me not to.

Even now, I remember it like it was yesterday. If that were to happen today, I might snap him in half. I didn't mention this incident to my parents; I was so humiliated that I told myself I would never allow somebody to do that to me again. And I haven't. I *have* almost messed up my underwear many times because of the fear factor in standing up for myself.

You must take a chance on yourself to change. If something makes you feel so uncomfortable, that something needs to change.

Change Your Actions

Life is an inventory of experiences. It's an inventory of memories, good and bad. I think a mistake many people make is they want to forget the bad and only remember the good. That's why social media is so exciting to people. It's fantasy, not reality. If you look at all the social media sites, you see snapshots of folks in their good moments. It's not real.

Take inventory with these questions:

- Do you want to change for the better?
- Do you want to be more compassionate?
- Do you want to be more understanding?
- Do you want to be more patient?
- Do you want to be more loving?
- Do you want to be a better spouse?
- Do you want to be a better parent?

If you want to make better decisions for yourself, you should go through your inventory. It will tell you all the things you did wrong, and that's okay. But if you don't look at everything you've done wrong, until you take your last breath, you will continue to make the wrong decisions.

Remember the decisions you make and don't repeat the bad ones. Work to repeat the good ones. That's how you evolve — not by pretending the bad things didn't happen in your life. Embrace the bad things.

If you can work on the bad things, it makes the good things that much better. It makes you that much better as a person because you're taking your weaknesses and slowly making them into your strengths. If you can improve your weaknesses a little bit, you know you will be pretty good.

Everybody in this world deserves better. You just need to acknowledge that you do. I'm sure you've heard stories of people in bad relationships. Sometimes this is because a person believes they don't deserve love, they don't deserve happiness. The relationship is so bad that it's like a shackle, and they feel they can't get out of it. But yes, they can.

If you're in a bad relationship, why do you think you don't deserve a good one?

If you're in a nowhere job, why don't you do what you need to get a *some*where job?

If you make bad financial decisions, either find a professional that can help you, or do the homework that is necessary to make better financial decisions.

Everything is changeable if you're willing to take your personal inventory honestly. Take ownership of it, then make decisions that are contrary to your past bad decisions.

It's going to be painful. It might even be humiliating. But it's going to be exhilarating once you do so.

CHAPTER TWO

Recognizing Examples of Your Programming

TRUST YOUR GUT

Have you ever decided something in spite of your gut telling you not to?

I think we do that all the time. We are each born with a unique intuition when it comes to the decisions we make about our personal and business relationships. But, many times we go against that intuition and make decisions contrary to what we feel we should. It's like an internal tug-of-war.

Sometimes we do this because we think it's what others want us to do. Sometimes we make a decision against our gut feelings because fear overcomes us. Sometimes we make these decisions based on what was modeled to us as children. But the people who taught us as we were growing up are biased because what they know is typically based on how they were brought up.

As an individual, why wouldn't you trust your intuition?

Your intuition is the main ingredient of who you are and what you can become if you own it, accept it, and trust it.

Why Question Yourself?

I have my BFA designation, Behavioral Financial Advisor, which is the study of why people make the financial decisions that they do. Often, people make impulsive decisions without thought. It's no different than when you're driving in your car and somebody cuts you off. You start honking your horn, you're shaking your fist, you're yelling; we've all been there — I certainly have.

You may see an item and purchase it without giving it any thought. Or perhaps part of you is telling you to buy it, and part of you is insisting that you don't really need it.

What voice do you listen to?

Sometimes you need to hit pause — I call it *freezing*. There are no rules in life that say you must make any decision today, this moment, this very second. The decisions that we make should be thought out.

It's no different if you get into a confrontation. There is no rule that says you should bark back at somebody or that you must engage. It's in the process of disengaging, whatever the current circumstances are, that you can gain control of yourself, your thought process, and your actions.

Second-guessing yourself is really about slowing down. Take whatever is in your head out of your head so you can make prudent, sound decisions in all walks of life.

If I Feel It, It Must Be So!

We cannot turn off who we are as humans. We know what our realities are. If we know it and we feel it, it must be true. It must be so. We have natural intuition, and we feel internally what we're going through. If what you're experiencing is uncomfortable or not wanted, it's about finding the courage to change your dynamics.

No rule on this earth states that you must do the same thing over and over regardless of the similar results. We can change our results. Take the time to understand what you're feeling, how you're feeling it, and what's causing it; then make an internal decision from that point.

Do you go with it because you like what you're feeling internally, or do you need to make a change because you don't?

If you ask yourself to consider this process, you can go to bed at night fully accepting the decisions you've made.

Accept Your Decision

Have you ever been let down by trusting the wrong person, or setting expectations so high that there was just no way possible that they could be met?

It's happened to all of us. For example, many of us have experienced a time when our eyes were bigger than our tummies, and we continued to eat in spite of needing to unbutton our pants.

The whole process of accepting your decisions in life starts with trusting your intuition. But, to open up the avenues of that intuition, you have to slow down, and you need to allow those doors to open. Get rid of the junk, the overexuberance, or the fear. These two steps go hand in hand.

Once you're able to slow down your process and understand what your gut is telling you, you will then understand why you feel a certain way so that you can better rationalize your decisions. If you go through a process in which you consider the questions at hand—for example, purchasing an expensive item or considering a job offer—you begin by doing your internal homework.

The practice of slowing down is preparation. One cannot prepare in a fast manner; it takes time, consideration, and thought about what you want the end goal to be. I've always used the example of going into a job interview — lack of preparation can rob you of an opportunity.

When I was much younger, I was told to go to the place of potential employment the week prior to an interview:

- Hang out in the lobby.
- Pay attention to how the employees dress.
- Try to eavesdrop on conversations.
- Ask questions of others.
- Research the company.

Today, you can Google the person who will be giving the interview. Knowledge is king and provides you the best opportunity for success. The same goes for your finances. Don't just trust what you hear — research it!

Once you go through this drill, you're emotionally prepared to make that decision. It will be so much better and easier to accept that decision because you took the necessary steps to slow down the process.

We are all flexible if we allow ourselves to be.

We all have value, if we accept it as such.

We all have the opportunity to improve our situations if we have the courage to do so.

When I meet with my clients, I hold a personalized seminar just for them and their needs. I take my time to make sure they understand my methodology and why I feel it is suitable for their financial goals. I *want* them to ask questions and to challenge me. That way, to the best of their and my ability, they are prepared for the financial journey we are heading toward. There may be obstacles along the way, but we are prepared for them.

Challenge yourself to be better by slowing down and going through the thought process. If you do, especially when it comes to finances, you will find that you can reach your financial goals, you can put your child through college, and you can retire with a better standard of living.

You just need to create a disciplined pathway that's based on trusting what your gut is telling you. I use a detailed process when meeting with a client for the first time. They talk, and I listen. I want to know what their *gut* is telling them.

Then I ask, "It's not only about what you want, but at this very moment, do you think you are on track to get there? What does your gut say?"

After having this detailed conversation, my staff and I create an overview from the thirty-thousand-foot level. We draft all the notations to make sure we have *heard* correctly what the potential client has explained. We then create a generic pathway. We ask the client to review it and confirm that we are all on the same page. At this time, we cover investment concepts and the risk and rewards of each.

Once the client understands the plan, we adjourn. My staff and I do our research to find the best solutions to fulfill this pathway. When the research is complete, we meet again to cover the specific investments that we will be using.

- Is it a long process?

- Are we prepared to cover all angles?

- Does our client have multiple opportunities to ask as many questions as possible during the process?

- And finally, upon completion and agreement of our financial solution, is the client much more prepared, knowledgeable, and confident than when we first met?

The answer to all these is — *absolutely, yes!*

This is so because we helped them slow down the process. We addressed their gut feelings and created a disciplined approach toward their financial goals.

RECALL EXAMPLES FROM YOUR YOUTH

In the financial advising industry, there is a phrase that states: *Past performance is not an indication of future returns.*

Experiences from your youth are in your past, but they are also future indicators that you must deal with as you move forward.

Experiences from your youth are the driving force of who you will be as an adult, and how you understand these past experiences and manage them internally are crucial.

Recollect Your Best and Worst Early Experiences

We all have heard the following phrases:

- *He was born with a silver spoon in his mouth.*
- *There are two kinds of people: the Haves and the Have-Nots.*

There are many more phrases, and often these beliefs are what we will carry into adulthood, both emotionally and in how we handle our finances. A perfect example could be if somebody grew up in a lower-middle class family without a lot of money. Maybe the parents were hardworking laborers, and one of them unfortunately suffered a layoff.

Maybe the stress from the parents came into the home and affected the child. Maybe they were told that the new sneakers they coveted couldn't be purchased because they couldn't afford them. On the flip side, when the parent finally found a new job and money was available again, the child got those new sneakers.

That was my situation growing up. My dad was that laborer; my mom migrated from Italy. They both worked very hard to put my sister and me through parochial school. I received one pair of tennis shoes a year. If those shoes got a hole in them before the year was up, I had to tape the hole. That will forever stay with me.

Back then, I didn't think twice about it. But to this day, I find myself being frugal even though I have achieved what many would consider a nice level of success. It's an example of a past experience that I brought with me into adulthood and that shapes how I manage money for my clients and my own investments.

I'm likely much more conservative than I would be if I had grown up in an upper-class environment and drove a new BMW in high school.

You take these things with you. You take expectations with you. My expectation is you need to work really hard to obtain what you want and hold onto it. These are early experiences.

The irony of all this is that while these are your experiences from childhood, you did not create them.

Many people who grow up poor work extremely hard so they never do without. Many people who are born into wealth fail to realize they did not earn that wealth—their parents did. When they become older, they have no clue how to duplicate that standard of living.

Those are the experiences of our youth that we take with us and that, as adults, we must manage and improve upon.

Close Your Eyes and Relive the Feelings

We are all computers. Our brain is a computer. Life experiences go into it, and our actions come out of it. When we think back to our youth, we have fond memories and some that are not so pleasant. Both have value in what we do as adults.

Maybe your parents bought you your first car because you got great grades. That demonstrates that your hard work can pay off. Then, maybe Dad lost his job, so you had to sell the car. You can learn from both experiences.

If you want to be accomplished, successful, and financially independent, you must deal in reality. You must learn from bad and good past experiences.

When I meet with clients, I want to know what makes them tick. I want to know what their best vacation was and why it was so.

Many times, clients will say: *Well, we saved our pennies so we could take our family on a beautiful vacation. It took us X amount of years to save for it, but when we did it, it provided memories of a lifetime that we will never forget.*

I find that empowering. That's being able to set a goal, commit to achieving the goal, and once you achieve it, to feel the joy of accomplishment and of creating memories that will be everlasting. That's why it's so important to look back, not through rose-colored glasses, but through realistic memories so you can create future realistic expectations for yourself.

What Would You Want to Duplicate?

Nobody wants to duplicate bad experiences, but you can learn from them. You want to duplicate the good things, the experiences that made you feel joyful and gave you a sense of accomplishment. It's such a rush.

For my client that took that vacation, it was almost like they were reliving it in the telling of it. The sparkle in their eyes, the joy in telling me the story, was priceless. Maybe they had a trigger point in their youth. Maybe it was their parents saying they would be rewarded if they did well in school. Chances are, they accomplished the goal.

Are you willing to do the work to get the reward?

If you didn't have that modeled to you growing up, how do you create that as an adult?

My story of the fear I felt at trying out for a part in the Edgar Allen Poe play is a perfect example of why you want to duplicate accomplishments. That was something I did not want to do—it was forced upon me by my teacher as a way to overcome my painful shyness. After I did it, even though I didn't get the part, it gave me a springboard away from being so frightened about trying something new, which led to not worrying so much about failing at other things in life as I got older.

That experience helped me come out of my shell; it helped me to develop a way to look inside of myself and recognized the fear. If I had given in to my fear, I probably wouldn't be where I am today.

Finance is the same way. People are often fearful:

- *I don't want to invest.*
- *What if the markets go down?*
- *What if the banks fail?*

We could play this game our whole lives, but:

- What are you basing these fears on?
- Are you basing these fears on the unknown?
- Have you done your homework?
- Have you done your research?
- Have you spoken to professionals?

If you become ill, are you going to lie in bed or see a doctor? Are you going to get information? Are you going to be prepared?

I bring preparation to my clients. I try to take the emotions out of it because my clients, like myself, are basing a lot of their decisions on past performances and on what happened to them as children. If my parents had lost their jobs and we lost everything, I would be scared, or at least cautious, when it comes to investing.

What happened to you as children may be the subconscious reason why or why not you came to see me. In any event, you are looking for assistance to make sense of it all. You are doing the work and seeking professional help. As a child, the financial circumstances are not of your doing but of your parents, both positive and negative. You may be the benefactor or may have done without in comparison to the other kids growing up around you. Ask the tough questions to give yourself a sense of comfort. Then, you can make an intelligent decision to improve your financial situation as you move forward with an advisor you trust.

The past can bring up feelings of joy, anger, sorrow, or guilt. Every one of those emotions is wonderful because it's a story that created a chapter of your life. Own your story. Accept it. Embrace it.

Always realize that even though these things happened to you in the past, it doesn't necessarily mean that you're a slave to these same experiences in the future. You can create your own future if you choose to, if you do the work, and if you look back and try to mimic the good and learn from the bad so you don't handcuff yourself into being stagnant.

Being ambivalent is the worst feeling that you can have. People who are stuck and stagnant are, in essence, ambivalent. They are going nowhere fast. One element in life will never stop and that's *time*. If you don't plan for your future, you're going to wish you had because you're not likely to experience what you had hoped for.

RELIVE THOSE EMOTIONS

Have you ever wondered who you are and how you got here?

Those are thought-provoking questions that I think people should ask themselves all the time.

At any stage in your life, you can reach a better understanding of yourself by asking:

- *Am I on track?*
- *Am I going in the direction that, years ago, I had hoped to be?*

If the answer is yes, that's great.

If that answer is no, do you ask yourself why not?

If that answer is somewhere in the middle, we have some work to do.

You need to take the necessary steps to move forward in life. But how do you do that?

In this section, I want to address the three avenues that I think drive us on a go-forward basis. If we don't recognize them, we can't manage.

Humiliation and Pain

The first part is thinking back to what really humiliated you and caused you a great deal of pain. It happens to us all. Nobody escapes childhood unscathed. Whether you've been bullied, people didn't understand you, or you weren't accepted, they are real and painful emotions. But that was then. This is now.

Subconsciously, do you let those instances in the past prevent you from confidently moving forward and trusting your decisions?

I find when I am faced with a major decision that my palms get sweaty and my heart races a little bit. I think back and ask myself why I'm so affected by making this decision, or I to talk to someone. If I feel anxious, I ask myself why. The anxiety may be triggered by a past event that was embarrassing or painful.

Consider that there may be an incident from your past that you haven't fully processed or accepted.

With instances of humiliation, you must marshal the ability to say: *I am not going to take it anymore.* If your parents were alcoholics, that doesn't mean you will be one as well. If you grew up in a broken environment, there is no rule that says you should create one yourself.

We learn more from the bad things in life than from the good. That is one thing I taught my children when they were growing up: You were born with gifts. You were also born with weaknesses. If you can acknowledge those weaknesses and work on just improving them a little bit, it will not only make your strengths that much stronger, but it will breed confidence as well. Overcome those obstacles of fear.

Joy and Love

You also want to embrace feelings of joy and love in your life. I personally feel that people, with few exceptions, are good. They want good things in life. They want good things for others.

The basis of humanity, as I see it, is not what you can do for yourself, but what you can do for others. If you think back to what brings you joy, chances are that those same things are what bring joy to others.

I have friends who, in spite of not being close to their parents, are great parents themselves. Parenting brings them joy and love.

Do you ever look in the mirror and say: *You know what? I really love myself.*

When working with clients, I often find that they're so caught up in the bad experiences in their lives they limit their true value.

What I tell people all the time is: How could you do well for others if you can't do well for yourself?

When you look in the mirror, only one person looks back at you. This is the person you owe, 100 percent.

If you're not good to the person looking back at you, how can you be good to your spouse, children, business, and finances?

You must be good to yourself first and foremost.

I look back at past painful experiences and I think: *Wow. That really sucked.*

But the experience doesn't put any kind of weight on who I am. I know I do my best to treat everybody with respect. I have friends and relationships from all walks of life, all nationalities, all creeds, and all sexual orientations because I look at each person as an individual.

- Are you a good person?
- Do you look at yourself and say the same thing?
- If you feel that you're limited by your actions, why not explore that?
- Look back at what made you feel the most joy and love — why not duplicate that for others?

The first step of being successful is liking yourself.

I have great conversations with clients, and I find they're at peace. They have accepted the bad things that have happened to them because they know their character prevents those things from changing who they are as people.

Sometimes bad things happen to good people.

Do you become bitter?

Try looking back and telling yourself: *I really like myself. I'm a good person. It was just an incident. I can overcome it. I will overcome it. I'll make the changes in my life to do so.*

It starts with loving yourself enough to overcome the bad things.

Swim Against the Current

We have talked about accepting humiliation and pain as a byproduct of what creates fear in us internally. We have also spoken about needing to love yourself to bring joy not only to yourself, but also to others.

We all have internal strife, no matter how hard we try to improve. We are programmed to be who we are. But we don't have to accept situations that are less than ideal; we need to try to improve them. It's no different than swimming against a current. If you want to get from Point A to Point B in life, especially financially, sometimes it feels like swimming against a current.

Are you willing to sacrifice to accomplish what you want?

I have many clients who come to me asking, "Dan, can I retire based on what I have?"

My first response is, "I don't know. What are you willing to do? How much do you need in retirement? Have you worked the numbers backward?"

You may decide that you want the same income when you retire.

What does that mean as far as how much you need to create as an asset that you will draw from as income?

Maybe it's a million dollars. Maybe it's $2 million. Maybe it's $5 million.

I would ask you to ask yourself these questions:

- Are you willing to do the work to save enough to create that income?

- Are you willing to swim against the current?

- Are you going to be disciplined enough to put monies away, maybe in your 401k, maybe in other retirement plans?

- Are you willing to do the work?

- Will you let humiliation and pain overcome accomplishment?

- Will you let your fear of discomfort get in the way?

- Do you love yourself enough to pay yourself first?

Visa, MasterCard, and American Express will not pay for your retirement. But your own savings plans will. The biggest mistake people make is that they carry too much debt. Often, it's because they want to feel good in the short term. But they're fooling themselves. They're using the joy and love aspect cosmetically. Whatever the purchase may be, it's because it makes them feel good in the moment — until they get the bill.

You should ask yourself if you really need to make the purchase now.

Or, should you take that money and put it away for your future?

That's how we kick the can forward. But don't fool yourself. People feel good the first few times they put on that new coat, but that feeling wears off quickly. Ultimately, it's just a coat.

Set a goal for your retirement. Put money away for your future and keep that objective in mind. Every time you put monies toward it, you're getting that much closer. That has a tangible feel to it. You can see it. You can see that you're getting closer to your goal. You can almost taste it. But, if you unnecessarily spend money, you are getting further and further from the prize.

Sometimes you just need to reboot. Look at your patterns. Maybe you're trying to soothe some pain in your life — you're looking for short-term fixes, such as a new coat, car, or shoes. But if you have that internal conversation, the joy, love, and sense of accomplishment you'll feel from achieving your financial goal will have you think twice about where you put your money.

Swim against the current. Understand why you do what you do by slowing down. Every goal that you set for yourself can be accomplished.

I have been an advisor for over thirty years, and I have helped hundreds of people reach their financial goals and move in the right direction.

I have met some wonderful people. I have also met some people who unfortunately are merely pretenders. They say they want to accomplish things, but they're not willing to do the things that successful people do to become accomplished.

Like I used to tell my children, if somebody says *you have potential,* that's the kiss of death. *Potential* is simply a label. It's a label placed on people who haven't achieved anything yet. We're all born with potential. We're all born with a clean slate.

Are you willing to overcome your fears, understand why you make the decisions that you make, and work with a professional who can help guide you toward your goals?

Are you willing to swim against the current to get there?

That is the basis of becoming successful.

CHAPTER THREE

Owning Your Decisions

FORGIVE YOURSELF

There's an old saying that the definition of insanity is doing the same thing over and over and expecting different results. It may feel like in all walks of life, whether in our emotional decisions, our monetary decisions, or our health decisions, we move on a predestined path; however, we don't have to stay on that path.

The classic example is making a bad decision, or multiple bad decisions, and blaming somebody else. Case in point: Somebody has let themselves get a bit overweight. They know they're overweight. Maybe they try to talk themselves into believing that they're not. But the moment that someone mentions their weight, they erupt as if they haven't acknowledged the fact.

When you're looking at all processes in life, especially financial, you need the ability to forgive yourself, to let past mistakes go. While you cannot change the past, you can own your poor decisions and take the necessary steps not to duplicate them.

If you don't hold yourself accountable to the past, it's a precursor to what is going to happen as you move forward. You need to accept these decisions, and you need to look for a financial advisor—someone who is going to help you reach your goals, as I do with my clients.

Book an appointment with yourself to improve. The first step is to look in the mirror and tell yourself: *I forgive myself for making bad decisions in the past. Starting today, I am not going to do that again.*

Oops, I Did It Again

People by nature are creatures of habit. There was a popular song that came out years ago by Britney Spears, "Oops! . . . I did it again." That song had a lot of traction because of the message that most people can relate to.

We have all done things and vowed to ourselves: *I am never going to do that again,* only to find ourselves doing it again.

How do you start the process of controlling your impulses?

The only way to do so is to have an internal dialogue. We all know intuitively what our strengths and weaknesses are. I know mine. It might go back to my upbringing and to my attending parochial school. I was brought up in an Italian Catholic household where we felt guilty if we didn't feel guilty. There was a lot of guilt growing up in my home; we were taught to always take care of people, and not let down our parents. While that is a wonderful quality to have, you tend to be taken advantage of.

Because of how I have been programmed, I really care about my clients as a financial advisor. I take personally what we talk about, the objectives and goals we have together, and the road map we create so they can achieve their desired level of financial success. It's a partnership.

If you find yourself making the same mistakes over and over, are you relying on the right people to help you out of that cycle of negative results?

The first step in not making the same mistakes is to have that internal dialogue, followed by finding a support system that can steer you in the right direction. Can you trust someone to help you?

Look in the Mirror

When I sit down with clients, I ask them:

- What are your financial goals and objectives?

- What has deterred you from achieving those goals?
- Why are you sitting in front of me today?
- What do you hope to gain?

Often, people will tell me:

- *I need a budget.*
- *I can't manage my own money.*
- *I don't know what I'm doing.*
- *I think I know what I'm doing, but I just want a second opinion.*

While there are all kinds of conversations with my clients in my practice, the brunt of what I do in these conversations is learn their process. I want to understand their successes and failures. We learn from both.

People fail to attach reality to their visions. But, we are who we are; we only need to recognize it by looking long and hard in the mirror. The mirror doesn't lie. There is only one person looking back with all the strengths and weaknesses staring right back at you.

If you make the same mistakes, own it. If you're a selfish person, admit it. That's the only way you can work toward not being selfish. If you're self-destructive financially, own that too. Nobody is forcing those decisions on you. When you come right down to it, your actions are straightforward. You must look in the mirror and admit it to yourself.

I Am Who I Am

Ask yourself:

- Do I respect the people in front of me?

- Do I only place value on what they can provide, or do I look at someone and think about what I can provide for them?

- Can I make their day a little better by simply engaging?

I've worked with doctors, attorneys, and physical trainers who I am paying to help me, but that doesn't mean I can't provide at least the courtesy of friendliness to their day. Do we make all conversations or actions about ourselves, or even when we're paying for it, bring some mutual humanity to both our processes? That can create a great experience and maybe a long-lasting relationship.

Typically, most new clients who come to see me initially interview me. But, as in most business relationships, it isn't one-sided. It must be mutually beneficial. When I take on a new client, I want them to know that I want them to be as vested in my success as I am with theirs. If we agree to that, then chances are we both will be successful — which is the perfect scenario for any relationship, both personal and business. I try to tell new clients that it's a mutual interview.

For myself, it was a long, arduous process to finally take inventory of the type of person I was at that time and the type of person I wanted to be. I've looked long and hard into that mirror, and I am who I am without apology. Without the resolve to want to challenge themselves to be the best they can be, most people don't go to that extent to understand who they are as a person.

Do you like yourself?

Are you the best person you can be?

You must answer those questions before you can improve.

You must acknowledge you like yourself.

You need to accept assistance.

You need to accept direction.

I'm still learning. I never think I have all the answers. Only a fool would think they do.

A basic exercise that we used to call the *Benjamin Franklin close* may be helpful. It's pretty easy. When faced with a decision, Benjamin Franklin used to write a large T on a piece of paper. Then, at the top of one side, he would write Pros. On the other side, Cons. Whatever the question at hand, he would go down and write all the pros, then the cons.[1]

You could do this exercise about yourself. What are the pros you feel that you possess? On the other side of the sheet, write the cons. It's a ledger. Look at it. Accept it. You are who you are. That way, you can start taking positive steps in changing for the betterment of yourself and your family.

When faced with a decision, such as *Should I buy that new car?* consider the pros and cons. Same thing around the question, *Should I buy that new house?* Or, *Should I stay in this relationship?* Examine the ledger when you're done writing; it should help with your decision.

I find I am my biggest critic. If I accidentally hurt someone's feelings, I am devastated. It really bothers me. Here's a perfect example: A friend's birthday was coming up, and a bunch of us were planning a big golfing getaway for him. I was really excited about it. Unfortunately, I let it slip out during a conversation,

---

1   *Mr. Franklin: A Selection from His Personal Letters.*
Contributors: Whitfield J. Bell Jr., editor, Franklin, author,
Leonard W. Labaree, editor. Publisher: Yale University Press:
New Haven, CT, 1956.

and I spoiled the surprise. I was personally devastated by it.

During the trip, I bought the most enormous seafood tower for about twenty people, which probably cost me $1,000. That was my guilt acting, which is essentially why I entered the financial advising field. I wanted to help take care of people.

While I made that mistake of spoiling the surprise, I owned it. Nobody made me open my mouth at that time. But, I tried to make it up to him, and I forgave myself. Being of Italian descent, sometimes we speak before we think, but I am who I am.

The reason I am telling you this is because it is perfectly okay to admit your mistake — to own it and to feel awful about it, but it also doesn't mean that you shouldn't make up for it especially if it affects others.

If you've ever hurt yourself or somebody else, own it, forgive yourself, accept who you are in the process — but more importantly, do something about it. It will make you and others feel much better not only about you, but also about the whole situation at hand.

YOU'RE BETTER THAN YOU THINK

As I have mentioned earlier in the book, I was painfully shy growing up. I had little confidence in myself.

It doesn't matter how many times a parent, a teacher, a coach, a friend says: *You know, you're a good guy,* or *You're a good gal;* until you believe it, it's not so.

Everybody has self-doubt. I don't care who you are. The most confident person on this earth has a little insecurity. I think if you take inventory of yourself, you will realize you're a lot better than you think you are. If only we can see in ourselves what others see in us.

Insecurities

While we are talking about insecurity, there's one thing our youth are faced with today that wasn't an issue for people of my generation and a bit older. We didn't have this constant blasting of information through the internet. We didn't have the constant multi-media noise going around. Today, cyberbullying is common. Body shaming and all the negative content and comments really affect people.

One thing people should realize is we all have insecurities. We have all done things that maybe we're not proud of. We have all either been humiliated or have taken part in humiliating others — or both.

I think it's tragic that kids and young adults now look to the internet as a way to be self-confident. But it's not reality. They allow words to hurt them. They allow past bad decisions to define them. This type of torment will continue to tear at you for the rest of your days if you let it.

If you grew up in a difficult environment and you are blessed with your own family someday, you don't have to duplicate it. You can learn from it. You can learn from your past, acknowledge it, and remember the pain, then go on to create the reality you want for yourself.

Positive Things Others Say About You

The most important things in life are your relationships. It doesn't matter how good your life is or how bad it can get — the difficulties we go through, the successes we achieve — because in the end, it's all about relationships.

Do you do your best to foster them?

I'll give you a perfect case in point. I value my clients. With the majority, I have become close friends. I care about what happens with them, their families, and their kids. We hold client events when we don't even talk about business. It's just a thank-you for our relationship.

Do you go out of your way to let the people who are in your life, both personally and professionally, know that they're of value?

That's how you have open conversations with people. You start developing a relationship of trust.

Without trust, what do you really have in a relationship?

I can tell you — it's not a relationship.

I think the only way to know what people really think about you is to have the guts to ask. I'm open with my friends. When we see each other, both men and women, we give each other a hug and we are open. I appreciate that.

They will tell the truth if I ask them: *What are my strengths and weaknesses?*

It's honest and pure. That's all you can hope to have in life.

An effort to understand yourself is a two-pronged attack. It's not only what you think of yourself, but it's also what others think of you. That is when you truly discover the positive things that others say about you.

Positive Things You Say About Yourself

We have already talked about forgiving yourself, understanding yourself, and learning from your past, but do you have the ability to look at yourself and say positive things?

Do you love yourself?

I have asked my kids, others who might be having issues both personally and professionally, and clients in my own practice: *What do you think about yourself?*

When I ask clients that question, they look at me confused at first because I am just their financial advisor. Aren't we supposed to talk about numbers only? I am trying to draw their attention away from numbers because numbers are sterile. They don't tell you a story.

The rate of return on an investment does not tell you the story of your goals and objectives or why you have the investment. Goals and objectives are unique to each individual, and that's the story I'm interested in hearing.

I like to find out something positive about each client. All of a sudden, it's almost like I can hear the brakes screeching because they have never before had that conversation with a financial advisor. It tells me so much about the person I'm dealing with. It tells me not only how to manage their finances but also how to manage their expectations.

What positive things do you say about yourself?

That's the precursor to success. That's what allows you to take positive steps going forward.

I think everybody would be better off if they just gave themselves a break. Slow down. Take it day by day because you don't know what tomorrow will bring.

If you wake up in the morning and tell yourself: *This is going to be a good day,* chances are it will be.

But if you hold onto the past, if you don't forgive yourself, if you don't fill your mind with positive thoughts, you're preventing yourself from moving forward in a positive way.

GETTING WHAT YOU DESERVE

Have you ever had something bad happen to you, and when you looked at the situation you thought it was somebody else's fault?

Sometimes that happens. But if something negative happens to you repeatedly, maybe you're the common denominator. You need to understand the pattern in order to change direction.

Creating portfolios is a puzzle. It's risk-reward. Life is the same way. There is a risk-reward to every decision we make in life.

Do I ask this person to get married or accept this marriage proposal?

It's a risk-reward. We know today that divorce rates are high, but we still take the leap.

Do I enter into an investment?

Risk and reward.

Prior to 2008, the housing market was rising at an unsustainable rate. People saw their home prices escalate — on paper. But then we had a major correction in the real estate and stock and bond markets.

What were people doing back then?

They were using their homes as their personal ATM machines, refinancing and pulling money out because the value of their homes went up $100,000 in a month. I saw very successful people become caught up in this frenzy and, in the end, lose their investments.

In an effort not to repeat past failures, you must own them. That's the only way you can learn going forward so you can prevent similar failures from happening again.

Own Your Unhappiness

Have you ever talked to a person whose glass is always half empty?

I have. I try to be as optimistic as possible. But when I'm around people who are negative, it slowly starts to turn my half-full glass into a half-empty one just by pure attrition of energy.

Like many of us, these people have had negative thoughts and been unhappy about particular situations, and they think that if that situation hadn't taken place, everything would have been better. That's not reality. Unhappiness comes from within.

As I've said, bad things happen to good people.

I'll apologize for what I'm about to say but, *get over it*. If something bad happens to you, do you have a pity party and sit there and mope? Moping won't change anything because what's the alternative? If you compound a bad situation and make it worse by shutting down, this causes you to pump your brakes. You can't go forward while you're having a pity party.

If your 401(k) dropped because the market dropped, and you were too aggressively positioned, or your investment went south because you jumped into it without doing any research simply because a friend told you it was a can't-lose opportunity, own your unhappiness. You made a bad decision. That's life.

Don't let it consume you. Take it for what it is — a lesson. Don't let short-term unhappiness turn it into a lifetime of pain and suffering.

You Deserve Happiness, Joy, and Love

As a financial advisor, I often have conversations with my clients about millionaires and multi-millionaires. Their thoughts typically range from being lucky to being born into money. Let's put it into the right context.

With respect to luck—let's say a lottery winner—well over 50 percent of lottery winners are bankrupt within five years of winning the lottery. They were given an opportunity, but they blew it.

Multi-million-dollar business owners have often experienced failed businesses and bankruptcy before reinventing themselves and hitting it big.

I tell people not to be envious of success; emulate the things that successful people do. You deserve success.

For example, we have all seen that couple who can't keep their hands off each other after many years of marriage.

It's annoying, right?

Wrong. That's wonderful. We can all work toward having that kind of relationship.

Couples need to work at bringing out the best in each other. Love your partner and love yourself so you can work toward having true happiness. Don't you and your partner deserve the very best in each other?

If you are not where you want to be financially, are you working toward it?

I tell this story a lot. I remember vividly when I was young growing up in East Los Angeles, which was a rough area. I used to visit relatives who lived in other areas and tell my mom that I thought they lived in the bright part of the city. What I didn't put together at the time is that I thought it was bright because it didn't have graffiti-covered buildings like my neighborhood did.

We had to pinch pennies when I was growing up. I used to tell my dad, "I want to have that fancy car someday."

And he would respond, "Dream if you have to dream. That's where it starts."

I wanted the nice things in life. But, I wouldn't have been able to get them if I didn't think I deserved them. I'm very happy now. There is a lot of joy in my life, and I have a wonderful wife. I have wonderful children and a wonderful family. I have wonderful friends too. However, life can be half full if you let it, but until you believe that you are deserving, what you want may never come.

Why Not You?

We have likely all wondered what it would be like to have that big house, the fancy car, and the great vacations. When I was young, someone taught me about visualization and asked me if I visualized success and accomplishing goals. I'll never forget this.

It's not enough to say you want something because those are just words you throw out there when nobody is listening. There is no accountability. I have been angry, and I have thrown curse words out there. It didn't hurt anybody because it wasn't directed at anyone. Conversely, I have thrown positive words out there, but again, there was nobody out there to listen to them.

When I was around twenty-two, somebody said, "Dan, cut out pictures of those things you want from magazines. Make a collage of the house you want, the kind of car you want, the kind of lifestyle you want. Put that as a Forever Memory that you can look at when you get up in the morning and when you go to bed at night. That will keep you honest and working toward your goals."

My mom used to say about my playing sports, "No one is better than you, but nobody is worse than you. Everybody puts their pants on one leg at a time."

Think about and visualize your goals. Maybe it's a retirement goal, or an incredible vacation you want to take. Look at yourself in the mirror before you go to bed at night, hopefully with a little smile, and ask yourself: *Why not me?*

When somebody comes to me with particular financial goals that they doubt they can achieve, I look them in the eye and say, "Why not you?"

As human beings, I think we are one incredibly large untapped opportunity, not only for ourselves, but also for everyone else. The barriers we erect in life are self-inflicted in most cases.

If you take the steps to invest in yourself, which I believe is the key, understand what makes you tick, forgive yourself for past mistakes, and admit that you may not be giving yourself enough credit, you will get what you deserve.

CHAPTER FOUR

Recognizing Your Weaknesses

THINK BACK AND STOP!

Do poor choices from your past haunt you at times?

I think an important process of moving forward as an individual and in making better decisions, whether regarding your relationships or your finances, is to think back to how those experiences made you feel. Stop and listen to your internal conversation about it.

While you may still remember those situations, it doesn't mean you will continue to relive and mimic them as you move forward. Part of improving your finances and yourself is to think back and simply stop before moving forward.

Recognize but Don't Relive

I think I have a particular characteristic of looking back at past failures often; I'm not sure if I was born with this or if I evolved into it. Whether it's a personal relationship or a bad business decision, I think back and recognize these experiences, but I have an uncanny ability not to relive them. I don't live in those past moments; I don't live in those past failures.

For example, I was previously married and divorced; I have two beautiful children from this relationship. Thinking back, I feel like the individual I was married to didn't exist because that chapter of my life has ended. At the time, I remember looking forward to moving on to the next chapter of my life; I was not stuck in the place of reliving my experiences with my former partner.

It's the same thing with my personal finances. Even as a financial advisor, I have made some poor decisions. While I think back and I recognize my errors, I don't relive them because I can't truly move forward if I do.

You Can't Change the Past

Self-doubt is something I believe we all have in varying degrees. Our insecurities tend to be based on what has already happened. The cold, hard fact is that you can't change the past, but you certainly can learn from it. Dwelling on past mistakes almost dehumanizes the experiences you've had that have caused you pain and frustration and may have caused self-doubt.

If you consistently think back and dwell on your life's bad decisions or experiences—regardless of whether they were initiated by others or you — it can stunt your growth because you have not let go of that pain or humiliation. Dwelling on the past acts as a subconscious anchor that can create self-doubt and fear.

I have had so many crazy things happen to me. My mom once told me, "Boy, with the things that have happened to you, you've got to be one of the strongest people I know." I laughed because why would I dwell on the bad things?

Dwelling on or reliving anything won't affect change today.

It's like the high school football star always talking about how great they were — we've all heard of *that guy* who was the best, toughest, but who cares?

Even if you were *that guy*, that's in the past, and what have you done for yourself now?

The same holds true if you were treated poorly because you were different, and others laughed or picked on you. Don't dwell on insecurity — let it go! You have the opportunity to create your own path; thus, dwelling on the good or bad from years ago bears no fruit of the labor you invest in yourself today.

I certainly don't dwell on the good things, so why would I put the bad things above the good things if they happened in the past?

I try to learn from them and not allow them to faze me.

Finances are the same way. Don't think back to the loss of a job, promotion, or bonus; that's the past. Unless you let that go it might just repeat itself. Chances are, if you own what happened in your past and accept it, you'll be ready to turn the page and create a new future.

Laugh About It

I feel humor is a lost art; we take ourselves too seriously. Our failures or the memories of them can recreate those anxieties. However, you can choose to see the humor behind the anxiety because I don't know about you, but I've never seen a laughing person look stressed.

Maybe it was lending money to somebody you knew wasn't going to pay you back, but you did it anyway. I'm sorry, that's pretty funny. You knew the end result, but you did it anyway. Why be upset at the person who didn't pay you back when you should laugh at yourself because you gave them the money in the first place?

Unless you laugh a little and bring enjoyment to your life, you're never going to be able to have success and happiness going forward. If you study the most successful people, they are typically happy with themselves and with those around them. Happiness really does make the world go 'round, just like pessimism doesn't.

Is your glass half full or is it half empty?

Because two people could look at the exact same situation in totally different ways and get totally different results from that point forward.

My challenge to my clients is to purge the past, take a look at all these things that may have happened to you, and laugh about it.

We are all creatures of habit. Often, our habits are based on what has happened to us in the past. As I said, my challenge to my clients is not to relive the negative impacts of their lives but to try to find the comical aspects because they certainly can't change what happened in the past, nor would they want to.

You want to embrace the past because your experiences — good and bad — have helped you become who you are today. But if you dwell on the past, you can't move forward. If you laugh about it, that gives you a springboard to change.

Think about it, stop, and don't forget to laugh about it.

WHO YOU WERE IS NOT WHO YOU ARE

Very few people are born with natural leadership ability and confidence. I was afraid of everything growing up. You couldn't get a word out of me. It got to a point where I challenged myself by asking if I wanted to continue to feel so shy and vulnerable, or if I wanted to acknowledge who I was and make a change.

This part of the book is all about recognizing who you were but not necessarily who you are now.

Recognition Is Power

I like to think back to where I was five years ago, ten years ago, thirty years ago, when I was in elementary school, and then plot a course.

If somebody who knew me in elementary school says to me today, *"Dan, you haven't changed a bit,"* I've failed myself miserably.

That means I didn't learn anything. I didn't recognize what my weaknesses were, and more importantly, I didn't take steps to improve upon them.

When it comes to changing habits and patterns in life, the first thing is to recognize who you are at any specific point in time. Own your weaknesses, which most people don't want to face. That's why a lot of people go to psychiatrists and counselors because it's a process of stripping yourself down and learning who you are.

I could argue that you know what your weaknesses are, but you may not have, or want, the ability to recognize them and admit them to yourself. The moment that you recognize your weaknesses, you're empowered. Recognition is power.

Change Is Good

The biggest hindrance to success is fear. Most people don't know what they're fearful of. I've mentioned in the past that I was shy and scared, but if somebody had asked me what I was scared of, I wouldn't have had an answer. If you recognize your weaknesses and you work toward changing them, change is good.

Studies show that successful people reinvent themselves or look to improve themselves every couple years.

Do you challenge yourself to change?

I love change.

Some people frequently change their hairstyle, the car they drive, or the style of clothing they like to wear. But, they have a difficult time changing themselves, which is arguably the most important thing anybody has that they can change. Changing who you are for the better is something that will benefit you for the rest of your life.

Grow Up and Smell the Flowers

Somebody stole my lunch.

Somebody took away my boyfriend or girlfriend.

I lost money in the stock market.

These are typical instances in all walks of life. Maybe you contributed to it. Maybe you didn't. Regardless, pull up your pants and move forward.

The biggest mistake people make that I've seen in the thirty-plus years of being a financial advisor is they hold onto bad decisions, bad influences, or bad situations. I ask every single person whether they laughed about how foolhardy they were when they made their particular bad decision. When they inevitably say it's unlikely they laughed, I remind them that years later they are still talking about it like it happened yesterday.

If that describes you, give yourself a break. Grow up and smell the flowers.

People have difficulty forgiving themselves. Because of that, they're in this continual spin cycle of crud. Once you make a bad decision, it likely can't be changed; your next decision will help you out of your current predicament, and so on.

Life is about making good decisions, and life is about making bad decisions. We're human; it's going to happen. I can't worry about what I can't control, but I can certainly worry about what I *can* control.

When you have that take-no-prisoner attitude and you look for sound advice, in my case financial advice, and you are working with somebody that you trust, together you can achieve your financial goals and objectives. If you are with the right advisor who understands your goals, chances are you are going to achieve those goals together.

But you can't do that if you're thinking about and living from a place of what happened in your past. There will be a disconnect between you and your advisor, which will create a long-term roadblock.

Purge the past, acknowledge it for what it was, laugh at yourself because of your mistakes, grow up, and smell the flowers.

You know what?

If you do that moving forward, life will start to smell pretty good. It is certainly better than continuing to pick up weeds.

In summation, the equation is fairly simple. People change if they want to. Conversely, sometimes people won't change. You have the power to recognize your past and who you were at that particular point in time in your life, but that certainly doesn't mean that's who you are today.

WHO YOU ARE IS NOT WHO YOU WILL BE

Barriers are made to keep people out. The most frustrating thing I see when I am meeting with my clients is the barrier they create for themselves. What people must realize is who they are doesn't necessarily mean it's who they will be forever. We all have the ability to be better: better husbands, better wives, better parents.

We also have the ability to be better financially if we commit to doing so. In this section, I will talk about my impression as a financial advisor on how to do just that.

Love and Trust Yourself

I think what people at times fail to understand is that we get what we feel we deserve. If you don't feel that you're deserving of moving up the economic ladder, chances are you won't.

If you continually find yourself in bad relationships because you don't feel you deserve better, well, guess what?

You won't attract a better relationship.

I think the first process of success in all walks of life is to love and trust yourself because you *are* deserving of good things. Nobody can make you do or feel a certain way.

You are the only person who has that power, yet how many times have you been influenced by others in both a positive and negative way?

As I've mentioned before, when you are brushing your teeth in the morning and you look in the mirror, there is only one person looking back at you. Before going to bed at night, while brushing your teeth and looking in the mirror, you still only see one person looking back at you.

You owe it to yourself to be the best version of yourself you can be. But unless you actually think about it, breathe it, and live it, it will never happen, at least not on a consistent basis. Typically, people who really love and trust themselves are the ones who are the most happy and successful.

Dare to Be Great

You see someone driving a fancy car, or you see a successful person on TV and you may wonder how they achieved their success. For example, the Kardashians are very successful. To their credit, they dare to be great. That's their intention, and they make it work.

My questions to you are:

- What is your intention?
- Do you dare to be great?
- Do you dare to be the best you *you* can be?
- Do you dare to make the best decisions in a thoughtful manner?

I'll be the first to admit I don't make the greatest decisions all the time. Maybe it's my Italian descent, but I can be pretty loud. What I try to do now is be loud internally — have an internal conversation, and if you listen to my wife, I'm pretty abrupt with my vernacular.

I like getting better. I like being a better husband. Do I succeed 100% of the time? No way, but I want to be better. I like trying to be a better father. I like trying to be a better financial advisor for my clients.

What is the alternative?

If you don't continuously push yourself to be better, or should I say, dare to be great, others will pass you by for the simple reason that you are not moving forward.

Positive Actions Versus Reactions

How we move forward in life is based on what fuel we give ourselves. Sometimes, we go through life wondering what happened. Sometimes we go through life making things happen.

If you want to make positive changes to your finances, the equation is simple.

Do you create positive actions or do you react?

A lot of times, people react instead of act. It's no different than an exercise program. Life is one giant exercise program.

Who doesn't want to be in better shape?

Who doesn't want to fit into that outfit they used to fit into so long ago?

The equation is easy. I must exercise and watch what I eat to be able to do so.

Conversely, what's the reaction?

If I don't do these things, I am buying bigger clothes. It's simple.

If I want to plan for retirement, I must take positive actions:

- Save consistently.
- Put my monies into the appropriate types of investments.
- Stay disciplined

These are all positive actions versus facing the reality that I don't have enough money to retire.

What is my reaction?

I need to continue to work for who knows how many years.

Part of life and successful financial planning is training yourself to act positively instead of simply reacting to what you have not done. That's how we move forward.

Challenge yourself. Believe in yourself. You are able to achieve wonderful things, but you can't if you don't believe you can. You have to like, or shall I say *love and trust,* yourself as a person first and dare yourself to be great.

Take all your good thoughts and pop the clutch. Put them into action. If you do not do this, you won't be any better off. You'll find yourself in the same situation you were in so many years earlier, but you'll be older.

Time waits for no one. Waiting is not a way of moving forward in a productive manner for yourself and those around you.

CHAPTER FIVE

Making Positive Changes for Your Future

OWN YOUR PATTERNS

There is a saying from longtime Major League Baseball player and manager Yogi Berra that goes: "It's déjà vu all over again." Sometimes we go into a setting, and it's almost like we've been there before. Or we hear a conversation and it's like we've heard it before. Or, we make a decision, and we can't stop ourselves from doing it over and over again. It's like déjà vu.

The process of making positive changes for your future must include, as we discussed, acknowledging your patterns. Positive change is not easy. If anything, making positive change is extremely painful because we are all creatures of habit.

It's a process of breaking down past habits and barriers on a consistent basis, which will help us make positive changes for the future.

Definition of a Crazy Person

The definition of a crazy person is in each and every one of us. We're all crazy. We all make the same mistakes over and over.

But how do we police those mistakes to create a positive future for ourselves?

Because we are all creatures of habit, at times we return to the behaviors that are easiest for us and make us most comfortable. But sometimes we hope for different results.

We do want to mimic those things that create a positive effect, a positive result. And when it comes to goals — which could be losing weight, planning for retirement, or wanting to plan for our children's college — we start off with good intentions. The next thing we know, we're having that extra scoop of ice cream. Instead of putting money away for retirement or college funding, maybe we go buy that new car we really can't afford or go on an expensive vacation.

Insanity is a series of making the same irrational-rational mistakes over and over, but expecting to get different results. We must own our craziness and almost laugh about it because there is no such thing as a not-crazy person. We're all crazy.

You need to not take yourself so seriously, own where you are in your life—flaws and all, and even laugh about it. It's your story. Your craziness is a great self-reflection on what you have gone through during your life; maybe what you have gone through was meant to happen.

Your craziness is a building block from which you can learn so you don't make the same mistakes time and time again. Owning your craziness can be a tragic comedy from which you can create a wonderful future for yourself.

Have Your Patterns Changed Over the Years?

As we age, we all go through an evolution to a certain degree, some more than others. As I've mentioned, when I was young I was incredibly shy and timid, not a big risk-taker. As I got a bit older, through sports I discovered my internal aggressiveness.

I went from being afraid to say hi to people to now speaking in front of hundreds, if not thousands, of people in training sessions and seminars. Now that I'm arguably older than middle-aged, I'm more confident than I was in my twenties. I'm more adventurous, as I want to be more accomplished. I don't want any regrets. My patterns have changed because I forced myself to change them.

When I meet with clients and we talk about wealth, we talk about creating wealth, we talk about the transfer of wealth, and we talk about income distribution. These may sound like buzzwords, but what makes the buzzwords work and what makes a goal a reality is taking a look at your patterns over the years.

Have you changed your patterns to the degree necessary?

The biggest deterrent to financial success is the inability to change — the tendency to fall back into old patterns. I am conservative by nature, including the way I manage my money. It's about risk versus reward. But I need to take a balanced approach.

When you run your life only looking for a reward, with the pedal to the metal, so to speak, you crash and burn. On the flip side, if you run your life only thinking about having one foot on the brake, you may never get anywhere. Slow and steady does win the race. It's a balancing act. I create balance with my clients.

Part of great financial planning, in addition to money, is lifestyle. Money is the end result of creating a lifestyle you want. The only way to get there is to take a long hard look:

- *What have been my patterns?*
- *Am I satisfied with them?*

- *Am I satisfied with those results?*

If you're not, once you understand that your patterns have not worked consistently, you can work on changing them.

It's Okay to Stop and Change

One of my favorite songs is "Stop! In the Name of Love" by Diana Ross and the Supremes. I have my own spin on that Diana Ross song. To be a happy, goal-oriented, and goal-achieving person, you have to stop in the name of love — for yourself. Stop and love yourself for who you are, your weaknesses and your strengths, and own and accept yourself. Nobody but you can make you feel one way or another.

Stop. Own. Accept. Then you can change.

Self-reflection is one of the best exercises. I am a creature of pattern and structure. My alone time is when I get up in the morning, go to the gym, and put my earphones on. I don't talk to anybody; I have internal talks with myself.

I reflect on what I've done well and what I've done poorly. I concentrate on what I've done poorly because I want to work on those things. For example, I may feel I need to work on being a better person, a better husband, a better father, or a better financial advisor. I am holding myself to a greater degree of accountability.

You can't do that if you don't self-reflect or take the time to wonder what happened so you can start to make things happen. That's what self-reflection does. It's admitting you're a little bit crazy. It's admitting you have some interesting patterns you'd like to change. That's how you get to the point where it's okay to stop and change who you are.

CLEAN THE SHEETS

Whether I'm traveling or in my own bedroom, I'm in my happy place when I see fresh linens and a nice fluffy pillow. I love it. Feelings of warmth, comfort, and cleanliness overtake me. Part of being successful is washing away the filth that has accumulated over time.

We have all done things, or been subjected to things, that are embarrassing to us. We have all done things that may be embarrassing to others. We need to give ourselves a bit of a break, take a bath, and clean the sheets; it's a great start to what you will become in the future.

Why Lie in a Dirty Bed?

There's always that one person in every group, whether it's a friend or relative, who seems to frequently say something that makes people think: *I can't believe you just said that.*

I believe that if you have nothing good to say, don't say anything at all, but we all know people who ignore this sentiment. And, if we're honest with ourselves, we may have also ignored it from time to time.

There is no such thing as walking through life without being a little catty, a little envious, or a little jealous on occasion. Those are negative thoughts. It takes more energy to play the victim and to be negative than it does to be positive. The proverbial glass is half-empty versus half-full is so true.

It's the same thing when it comes to your finances. Just because you might be economically disadvantaged today doesn't mean that's what your tomorrow should be.

But if you don't have the ability to wash away those thoughts, how are you going to move forward in a positive way?

Progress of any kind, or the lack of taking that positive step forward, is much like lying in a dirty bed. It feels disgusting. If you consider yourself a pessimistic person or expect the worst, it's time for you to clean your sheets. If you don't, you are always going to lie in a dirty bed.

Get a Good Night's Sleep

Sometimes I find I just can't get to sleep at night. You probably have felt the same way. It could be because of any one of the stresses of life. Your mind gets into a constant spin cycle that you can't turn off. It is helpful if I acknowledge what I'm spinning about and what is keeping me awake. I have an exercise I think works well that may work for you too.

Being in practice for as long as I have, I've had the opportunity to help hundreds of people. I have also seen some unfortunate circumstances. I am continually living other people's successes, failures, and tragedies, and I am also doing the same for myself and my own family.

How do I get a good night's sleep when I am going through the junk email of my mind?

I stop, take a big breath, and think about all the things I'm fortunate to have. Most of the things that keep us up at night are things we really have no control over.

When I do this exercise, I consider the blessings that are my children. I also feel blessed because of my wife.

I think about my own parents and how fortunate I am that I had them. I go down this list, which takes me from that half-empty, crazed, I can't turn off energy to a more calm and tranquil state of mind. Then I can get a good night's sleep.

When I take that step, I sleep well. Now, you can't help your subconscious mind. I'll sometimes wake up at two or three in the morning spinning like a top. I get up, get a drink of water, come back to bed, and start that process. The next thing I know, my alarm goes off.

When I take a client through exercises, I don't talk in too much detail about what they don't have because that will keep them up at night.

My questions to clients are:

- What keeps you up at night?
- What are you thankful for?
- What was your favorite moment that you can look back on and the thought brings a smile to your face?

As my question progresses, I feel the energy of the meeting change.

Then I leave them with:

Don't let the day to day *junk* that surrounds all of us keep you up at night. Take what you're thankful for to bed at night and turn all that negative energy into a more calming and thankful state of mind because that's how you get a good night's sleep.

Wake Up Feeling Energized and In Control

Understand that sometimes bad things happen to good people. Life happens. But don't dwell on the things you can't control; look toward the things that you can. The only things you can control are your state of mind, your actions, what you want to accomplish, and the kind of relationships you want to build.

If you always focus on the positive and are thankful for what you have, how can you not wake up feeling energized and in control?

This leaves you focused on what you can control and takes the focus away from the negative energy of what you can't control.

I can't make my children make good decisions. They make the decisions they want for themselves.

Why would I lose sleep over that?

I worry about them all the time, but they learn from their decisions — good or bad. Similarly, I make decisions for myself and I am sure no one is dwelling on what it may be. However, with those decisions, whether it be good or ends up being bad, they are mine to own and learn from… no one else's.

There is a big difference in wanting to be in control and being in control. When you gain control of yourself, your relationships, and your finances, you wake up every day energized and looking forward to the day and what you can accomplish.

Mistakes and poor decisions are like barnacles that attached to us. We try to scrub them off, but sometimes they just stick. That doesn't mean you succumb to them. If you want to be successful and accomplished in life, you must mimic what successful, accomplished people do. We all make mistakes. Own them.

We all go through the spin cycle where we can't get a good night's rest. That's okay. Don't put pressures on yourself that are negatively influenced. Take a step back. Don't be overcome with worry, especially over things you can't control. You can't control the what-ifs.

When you start changing the process, cleaning the sheets, being in a happy place when you're going to bed, you're going to be in control. Every sheet you lie on from that point forward will be clean and hopefully leave you invigorated for a new day.

FREEZE — DON'T MAKE A MOVE!

We have all seen those old Humphrey Bogart or James Cagney movies where there is a cop trying to track down the criminal, and they are yelling, "Freeze! Don't make a move!" If we took those five words and used them toward ourselves, things would go a little smoother.

The way I look at it, we're not only the police, we're also the criminal in our own life. If we can slow down our impulsions, we just might limit the poor decisions that can come back to haunt us. Remember, there is no rule that states just because you have a thought, you need to act on it. Take a breath. Slow down!

Feel, Felt, Found

So far in this book, as you can tell, I've been talking more about the emotions and the psychology of accomplishment, or lack thereof. I haven't spent a lot of time talking about economics because anybody can turn on the news. We are all bombarded by economic news 24/7. If you listen to five different economists, you will hear five different opinions on what the economy will be doing. The facts are we're in a global environment and what happens domestically may or may not affect what happens in the international markets and vice versa, but realizing that in some way they are all tied together can help with a diversified approach to investing. With that being said, having an understanding of how the markets work is vastly different than how you may or may not take advantage of it emotionally.

As mentioned, I proudly hold the designation of Behavioral Financial Advisor. My job is to make sense of it all but not over- or underreact to the data that comes to us every minute of the day.

Everything in life that you're faced with can fall under a basic script. We have all had conversations that may have turned into heated arguments. You become heated and the person you're talking to gets heated, and the level of anxiety goes up because you're yelling and they're yelling, and the next thing you know it's like two crazy people yelling at each other and nobody knows what anyone is talking about.

Do you have that same conversation with yourself?

Here's a perfect example. I used to road rage like crazy. If someone cut me off, it was a good thing there were no children in the car because who knows what would be flying out of my mouth.

We need to slow our internal thought process down. When I train advisors, I tell them that when somebody gives them an objection—because not everyone will agree — acknowledge it. They have their own objections in life. Acknowledge them.

The way I do this is with three words: *Feel, Felt, Found.*

Feel. Do I acknowledge how I or someone else feels?

For example: *Hey Jim, I feel what you're saying, and just to make sure I am understanding you correctly, I want to restate your question.*

Now I am acknowledging how the other individual feels. If I am going through this for myself, I'll stop and think it over once, if not twice, so that I acknowledge what I'm feeling at the time, whether it is anger, sadness, or another emotion. After this, I have acknowledged how the other person or I feel at that moment and have not minimized anything. If I acknowledge the feeling, I am not reacting.

Felt. Then I can start the process of an answer:

Joe, I understand what you feel, but I felt this way.

This brings the level of anxiety down. How do I do it internally?

I know what I'm feeling, but now that I have slowed down my process I examine what I have felt. For the other person, I have brought down if not slowed down their level of potential anxiety.

In the case of somebody cutting me off, they're not affected so why am I letting that make me crazy? Why am I turning beet red, my eyes popping out of my sockets? That person that's driving away has no clue about my anger and is probably thinking about what kind of dinner plans he or she has.

Found. When I acknowledge the found part of it, I am stating my case. In talking to another, I can simply give a non-emotional answer. In my case, I have slowed my thought process to the point of not overreacting. If I am stating my case to somebody else, then it's up to them how they acknowledge it. But I am not yelling. I am not dictating.

If you're going off the rails, why are you doing so?

If somebody cuts you off, so what?

You didn't crash. Yes, it's frustrating, but it's not going to affect your life.

Feel, felt, found is an acknowledgement process that calms you down, keeps you from overreacting, and allows you to go on with your life. There is no reason to get too wrapped up in the small frustrations of life.

In a society where most of us overreact, don't be a part of it. It's no different than when a person posts something emotionally on the internet, then once they calm down, they quickly try to take the post down.

Maybe if they had an internal dialogue they could have prevented embarrassment to themselves. Slow down. You will be amazed at how much you can accomplish by slowing down and not overreacting.

No Scenario Is Greater Than You

We're all faced with different challenges in life, but how we meet those challenges and face our losses matters. Maybe you're facing the death of a loved one or a divorce. I've gone through both. As daunting and painful as these experiences are, we all need to learn how to move on and not let those experiences cripple us.

I've experienced a lot over the years. Some of these experiences have been extremely painful, but these experiences are not greater than I am. Each one of us is in control of our level of success or of failure. When people are overcome by their experiences, the experiences become a part of who they are.

Realize you have value, that you're a good person (hopefully), and that if you treat other people like you want to be treated (the Golden Rule), you can overcome just about anything.

Some clients were very wealthy, and through an event that was out of their control, they lost all their wealth.

But they had the right attitude, and they recreated themselves and their wealth.

Good friends of my family went from having it all — truly living an unbelievable lifestyle — to losing almost everything. During their most pressing times, they made some incredibly difficult financial decisions to cut their expenditures dramatically. Through it all, they never had a pity party, asked themselves, *Why us?* or changed their dispositions.

Because of their attitude, I am one of their biggest cheerleaders. They have reinvented themselves and are once again among some of the most successful people I know. They've proved that truly no scenario is too great to overcome both emotionally or financially.

The key is realizing that as long as you have your health, family, and good friends, whatever is thrown in front of you is just stuff. It's how you react in these tough situations that will determine how quickly and successfully you triumph over the hardships.

You Are Truly Blessed

Many people want to escape reality. My reality is that I'm getting old! I'll be the first to admit, and probably my wife would as well, I don't have the same body I had years ago. I laugh about it. I find aging comical.

Every wrinkle that appears tells a story. Every bad thing and good thing in your life is a chapter of a book. Every relationship you've had and lost or continue to have, and everything in between, helps define who you are today and in the future.

We need to realize that we are all truly blessed. I'm truly blessed for having the father I had. He passed away quite a few years ago, but I think about him every day. I'm blessed because of my mother, whom I treasure with all my heart and who is in ill health. I pray she lives long enough to read this book. I hope the same for my wonderful sister, incredible wife, awesome children, relatives, and friends.

I'm blessed with great relationships and with clients who are also dear friends. These relationships make me better. I care about my clients, and I'm invested in their success.

I try to be the best husband I can be. I know I'm not perfect — at least that's what my wife tells me (kidding), but that's okay. I try my best and so does she.

We live in a reciprocal environment. If you throw negativity, you will only get negativity back. But if you throw positive energy into the world around you, if you take positive steps for yourself, it's contagious. It's contagious for you and for those around you. The only way you can become accomplished is to realize that, at the end of the day, you are truly blessed.

Slow down. Enjoy life. Count your blessings.

I find that some of my most wonderful times are at a dinner table surrounded by family and friends. When I first became a financial advisor, I was running around trying to build a business so I missed out on a lot during that time.

Many of my clients are young executives, constantly on the go. Others are knocking on retirement's door, and they are worried. Then I have clients who are retirees, and they are worried about running out of money.

Whatever stage in life you happen to be in, stop! Freeze. Don't make a move. Have that internal talk with yourself.

What do you feel?

What's the felt portion of it?

Have that slowed-down conversation about what you have found. Also, realize that these fears are often self-inflicted. Ask yourself whether the fears are realistic. Just slow down. Have a conversation with yourself about it.

Start taking positive steps toward getting what you want and don't succumb to the fears or live in a state of negativity.

Be grateful for what you have.

Be thankful for who is in your life.

Everything will work itself out if you just put one foot in front of the other.

Everyone has the potential to reach their financial and personal goals.

Take inventory of what you have and what you want.

Be positive in your actions and you will reach your goals.

Conclusion

Average people can do great things. Everybody puts their pants on one leg at a time. You are capable of achieving any goal you set your mind toward.

Start thinking more positively, and imagine you have what you desire. Negativity should never be part of anyone's vernacular.

Instead, say things like: *When I . . .* and *Why shouldn't I . . . ?*

Get accustomed to using positive language, and create a series of mini goals to get to your end goal. Too many people put the carriage in front of the horse. You're the horse. Ride your own energy toward your path of success, whether it's in your relationships or in your finances.

That is the summation of everything.

Make it okay to fail. One of the biggest reasons people fail is they fear the failure itself. If I wanted to guarantee failure, then I'd never try or change the patterns that are giving me negative or undesirable results. Consider failures to be just another step on the road to success. If you are striving toward your goals, there may be momentary setbacks. If you want to have the opportunity not to fail, you must act.

Instead of sitting around wondering what happened or why it happened, why don't you make things happen?

Be true to yourself. Own your future. I think too many people are waiting for the future to happen instead of going out and owning what that future could be.

For a lot of people, aging is a process that terrifies them. I look at it as a new chapter to be embraced, to own, and to experience. It's your opportunity to write a new chapter in the book of your life.

Don't be afraid of change and don't be afraid of the future. Embrace it, and take positive steps, because we only have one life.

Granted, for most of us, we hope we go to a more beautiful place. Enjoy the ride until you get there.

Next Steps

Challenge yourself to change for the better. Beyond the financial benefits, positive change will bring about confidence and emotional satisfaction.

Share your thoughts with me via email at Change_is_good@elitefinancialnetwork.com.

For those who are interested in working with me directly after reading this book, please know that I will donate 10 percent of my earnings from new clients to St. Jude's Children's Research Hospital or our veterans.

About the Author

For Dan Cairo, helping people attain their personal and professional financial goals is rewarding work. As president and founder of The Elite Financial Network, Inc. (EFN), Dan takes a comprehensive and holistic approach to financial consulting.

Holding a Behavioral Financial Advisor™ designation, a complete plan involves understanding all aspects of your life even if you already have some of the pieces in place. He sees his role as helping people make well-informed decisions about their finances. His goal is to help individuals understand their emotional behavior toward finances and avoid major financial setbacks, simplify their financial lives, and achieve confidence in their investments.

With over thirty-two years of experience in the financial services profession, Dan is an experienced advisor in behavioral financial consulting and wealth management. He is also the registered principal for EFN and has put together a team of financial services professionals to provide clients with comprehensive planning that examines taxes, cash flow, insurance, estate planning, retirement planning, and investments.

The Elite Financial Network not only assists individual and corporate clients, but also serves as an information center for their investment consultants statewide, helping them help their clients reach their financial goals. Clients of EFN take comfort in working with a team of professionals who can take care of all their financial needs.

Dan lives in Huntington Beach, California, with his wife, Cindy; their children, Austin, Adam, Karina; and the Cairo mascots Roxy, their Wheaton terrier, and Casper, their multi-poo.

As parents, they are very active in the lives of their children and realize that children are a gift that we have only for a short time. Love them, support them, and invest emotionally in their future.

www.ingramcontent.com/pod-product-compliance
Lightning Source LLC
Chambersburg PA
CBHW071148200326
41519CB00018B/5158